THE IMPACT OF TECHNOLOGY IN
ART

Alex Woolf

heinemann
raintree

Edited by James Benefield and Amanda Robbins
Designed by Steve Mead
Original illustrations © Capstone Global Library Ltd
Picture research by Tracy Cummins
Production by Helen McCreath
Originated by Capstone Global Library Ltd
Printed and bound in China by RR Donnelley Asia

19 18 17 16 15
10 9 8 7 6 5 4 3 2 1

Library of Congress Cataloging-in-Publication Data
Cataloging-in-Publication Data is available at the Library of Congress web site.

ISBN 978-1-4846-2635-1 (hardcover)
ISBN 978-1-4846-2640-5 (paperback)

This book has been officially leveled by using the F&P Text Level Gradient™ Leveling System.

Acknowledgments
Alamy: LHB Photo, 37, redsnapper, 16, Steve Hamblin, 19; Anne Cleary and Denis Connolly/www.connolly-cleary. com: 36; Aurora Robson: Photo Marshall Coles, 25; Bathsheba Grossman: 22; Bridgeman Images: Alinari, 27, 30, Angela Easterling, 44; Corbis: Hero Images, 38; Dreamstime: Sébastien Bonaimé, 24, Softdreams, 17; Getty Images: AFP, 42, Bernard Gotfryd, 9, Bill Roth/Anchorage Daily News/MCT, 20, Fred W. McDarrah, 32, Gonzalo Azumendi, 6, JTB Photo/UIG, 39, Manjunath Kiran/AFP, 47, Matthew Lloyd, 5, 35, MJ Kim, 7, William Foley/The LIFE Images Collection, 43; Joseph Nechvatal: 13; Newscom: CHROMORANGE/H. Richter/picture alliance, 15; Shutterstock: Artishok, Design Element, Danil Nevsky, 11 Right, design36, Cover Top Right, Dragan85, Design Element, Dream79, 28, Iulian Valentin, 29, karakotsya, 40, kuznetcov_konstantin, 48, Cover Top Left, sainthorant daniel, 4, style_TTT, Design Element, wavebreakmedia, 11 Left, Cover Bottom, Yuriy Vlasenko, 41; Simon Colton: The Painting Fool, 49; Thinkstock: cnrn, Cover top middle, PanosKarapanagiotis, 8; Ursula von Rydingsvard: Courtesy Galerie Lelong, New York, 18; Yasuaki Onishi: reverse of volume RG, 2012/Commission, Rice University Art Gallery, Houston, Texas/Photo: Nash Baker © nashbaker.com, 21.

We would like to thank Alistair Ashe for his invaluable help in the preparation of this book.

CONTENTS

Some words are shown in bold, **like this**. You can find out what they mean by looking in the glossary.

ART'S TECHNOLOGICAL REVOLUTION

1

Artists have always made use of technology to create their work. Prehistoric cave painters blew paint through hollow bones to create an **airbrush** effect. The 18th-century artist Canaletto made paintings with the help of a camera obscura, a device used for projecting an image of a scene onto paper. Technology in art has made great leaps in the past few decades, particularly with computer and digital technology.

In this book, we will look at how technology has influenced the visual arts, such as painting, sculpture, photography, video, and printmaking. We will also look at new forms of art that have been imagined using technology.

⌃ The simple technologies of brush and paint remain as popular as ever among today's artists.

New formats

For centuries, drawing, painting, printmaking, and sculpture were the only **formats** through which artists could express themselves. This changed with the invention of photography (1830s) and filmmaking (1880s). These weren't immediately recognized as art. Many people felt there wasn't skill involved in pointing a lens at something and pressing a button.

Over many years, photography and filmmaking have become recognized as major art forms. They have also become less expensive and easier for artists to use. Since then, other technologies have been adopted by artists. Each time this happens, it challenges us to think again about what art is.

>> Minmaform's "Petting Zoo" uses technology to create an interactive experience. The "creatures" respond to people's movements.

The digital revolution

We are currently undergoing a revolution as big as any in the history of art, and much of this is a result of the rise of the computer. Digital technology has given visual artists an amazing range of tools, and art is now growing far beyond the traditional art forms. While many artists still use the traditional methods, they are also combining different forms and incorporating technologies such as **virtual reality**, **lasers**, and 3-D printing.

PIONEERS

DEVART

In 2014, Internet company Google launched a project called DevArt, **commissioning** young artists to "use technology as their canvas and [computer] code as their raw material" to create original, interactive works of digital art. The artworks were displayed at London's Barbican Centre during the summer of 2014, in a show called Digital Revolution. DevArt aimed to "push the boundaries of what is possible when art and technology come together." In one piece, called *Wishing Wall*, by Varvara Guljajeva and Mar Canet Sola, visitors were invited to whisper a wish into a microphone. Their words appeared on a screen and then curled up into a scroll before re-emerging as a butterfly.

Redefining art and artists

The increasing role of technology in art has started to change the meaning of art for many people. Traditionally, art is a work of technical skill and imagination, created with the aim of impressing people with its beauty or emotional power. For centuries, artists worked with their hands and minds. This meant having **manual** skills—for example, being able to use a paintbrush or a hammer and **chisel**.

Today, art is all about the final product and not always about the process of achieving it. Some artists have a vision, and then they use technology, or hire technical people, to help create it. Some artists make their art using computer software, which also requires both skill and artistic talent.

TECHNOLOGY THROUGH TIME: ARTISTS WORKING TOGETHER

People with different artistic talents have **collaborated** with one another for hundreds of years. In the late 15th and early 16th centuries, artists collaborated to produce the decorations for the Sistine Chapel in Vatican City, Rome. Artists and their students produced 12 large frescoes, and Michelangelo spent three years painting the famous ceiling. Artistic collaboration continues today. For example, an arts organization called Rhizome brings together artists and technologists in an annual event called Seven-on-Seven. Seven technologists are paired with seven artists over a period of 24 hours and asked to develop a new work to present to a live audience.

Conceptual art

This move away from manual skills began in the 1960s, with a movement called **conceptual** art. The conceptualists believe that the concept, or idea, is the most important aspect of an artwork. This means that how the work is made, and even who produces it, is less important.

As technology has advanced, some art has become even more conceptual. Many artists are teaming up with technologists to bring their visions to life. Of course, many artists continue to make art using traditional methods, including famous ones.

CASE STUDY

DAMIEN HIRST

For the Love of God (2007) is a platinum sculpture featuring a human skull covered with over 8,000 diamonds. The idea for the artwork came from the artist Damien Hirst. Hirst did not make the object, though. After Hirst had this idea, the work was designed and sculpted by jewelry designer Jack du Rose and was manufactured by the jewelers Bentley & Skinner.

CASE STUDY

JUST FOLLOW THE INSTRUCTIONS

Some conceptual artworks, often called installations, can be simple enough to be created by anyone following a set of instructions. For example, conceptual artist Martin Creed won the Turner Prize in 2001 for an installation called *The Lights Going On and Off*. It featured an empty room in which the lights went on and off every five seconds.

2 PAINTING

Humans have painted pictures since prehistoric times. Cave paintings in Malaga, Spain, may be more than 40,000 years old. People throughout history have painted for different reasons:

- In ancient times, artists were commissioned to glorify the powerful, demonize enemies, honor the dead, or beautify buildings with scenes from myth and legend.
- Religious art flourished during the Middle Ages.
- More recently, painting has become a form of artistic self-expression.

Prehistoric pioneers

Our prehistoric ancestors invented the basics of painting. Paleolithic cave painters used earth **pigments**, such as charcoal. They ground these into a paste, mixed them with animal fat, and applied them with brushes made of animal hairs, plants, or twigs. Everything that followed—until the arrival of digital painting—simply refined the techniques created by the cave painters.

This ancient Minoan fresco has been restored to show the original bright coloring. The fresco technique allowed color pigments to be applied to a wall without the need for a binder.

Art in ancient civilizations

The Egyptians added blue and green (made from copper minerals) to the prehistoric **palette**. The Minoans invented fresco painting: applying paint to wet plaster walls so the paint soaked in and became a permanent part of the wall. The Phoenicians gave us purple, from the mucus of a sea snail, and the Aztecs gave us crimson, from crushed beetles.

Painting through time

In the 14th century, Italian painter Giotto (full name Giotto di Bondone) began using egg tempera (a mix of water and egg yolk) as a **binder**. This achieved a clearness and brightness of color unknown until this time. In the 16th century, oil became a popular binder. Oil dries more slowly, and with it, artists can achieve more intricate effects.

By the 19th century, paint-making had become industrialized. Manufacturers produced pre-mixed paints in tubes, which artists could carry around with them. Advances in chemistry had led to the development of a huge variety of colored paints and dyes.

With the rise of the personal computer, a completely new way of painting arrived. Instead of applying paint with a brush on canvas or paper, artists could now use computer software and digital tools.

TECHNOLOGY THROUGH TIME: COMPUTER-PAINTING SOFTWARE

1963: Sketchpad, the earliest computer illustration program, is launched. This enables users to create simple shapes, such as lines and circles, on a screen.

1964: The RAND company develops the first commercially successful **graphics** tablet—a device that **digitized** images drawn on its surface with a **stylus**.

1984: MacPaint, launched by Steve Jobs's company Apple (see picture, right), allowed artists to create simple digital color paintings. These paintings can be copied and pasted into other documents.

1987–1990: Adobe introduces Illustrator in 1987 and Photoshop in 1990, enabling more sophisticated effects. Illustrator and Photoshop remain the most popular programs used to create digital paintings. They are also used to help alter photographs.

A flexible tool

Computers offer artists a degree of flexibility well beyond anything possible in traditional painting. Artists can use a graphics tablet and stylus or finger-paint directly onto the screen and do many things:

- The screens are pressure-sensitive, allowing the artist to vary the intensity of the stroke.
- Artists can mimic oil paints, watercolors, pastels, charcoal, pen, or even airbrushing.
- They have an available palette containing millions of colors and can choose almost any size of canvas.

Special effects

Artists can achieve special effects using computer software. Artists can choose the style and size of the brush; softness or hardness of the brush; and whether they want to produce a smooth or speckled look.

In addition to these traditional art effects, digital painters can also produce results that are difficult or impossible to achieve otherwise. These include repeating objects (using a copy-and-paste function) or making them transparent, perfectly symmetrical, geometrical, or 3-D.

Digital paintings are created in layers that can be individually edited, so artists can add, remove, or change them without affecting the rest of the painting. This allows for experimentation. For example, an artist wishing to see how a painting looks with highlights could examine it with and without the highlights before deciding which is better.

THE SCIENCE BEHIND: DIGITAL PAINTINGS

The content of a digital painting is stored in fixed rows and columns of **pixels** on the computer's hard drive. Each pixel contains values in terms of color, brightness, and intensity. When a pointing device, such as a stylus, moves over the image, new colors and values can be applied to the pixels it touches. Some painting programs use vectors rather than pixels. Vectors are representations of shapes.

FOR AND AGAINST DIGITAL ART

FOR

Digital painting software allows artists to work in an organized, mess-free environment. They no longer have to carry their supplies around with them if they want to paint outside the studio. They can whip out their tablets, open a program, and use their fingers as brushes to create instant works of art. Artists like this freedom because it's so immediate—they can capture a moment as it happens.

AGAINST

When you look at a traditional painting, you know that it contains within it the full story of its creation. Every line and color was put there personally by the artist. Individual brush strokes may even be visible. And if there are mistakes or imperfections, they are recorded there, too. The artist wasn't able to backtrack or delete mistakes, as a digital artist can. It could be argued that this makes traditional paintings more **authentic**.

⌃ You can use your tablet anywhere. It doesn't have to be at a desk.

⌃ You could lose some of the quirky imperfections of art if you just go digital.

The problem of uniqueness

When an artist completes a painting using traditional methods, only one version of that painting exists. It is unique, and therefore it has value. The buyer knows that he or she is buying the only version of that painting.

The same cannot be said for a digital painting. Once completed, the painting exists as a computer file. It can be printed out or shared across the Internet. This lack of uniqueness gives digital art less value, and this is why digital paintings tend to sell for less than traditional paintings. As more artists go digital, this could have a major effect on what kinds of art people want to buy.

Standard Certificate of Uniqueness

Some digital artists have tried to protect the uniqueness of their work by issuing a Standard Certificate of Uniqueness. This is a promise to the buyer that:

- only one **physical** form of the work will be created
- to identify it as the artist's work, the artist will imprint his or her fingerprint in wet paint on the front of the printed painting
- the buyer has the **exclusive** right to sell the work
- the artist will delete the original digital file.

Computers as tools

Digital paintings are created using a computer as a tool. But there is another kind of art in which computers play a more central role. With computer-generated art, a computer creates an image according to an algorithm (a set of pre-programmed rules).

To prevent the computer from reproducing the same image again and again, the artist inserts an extra element into the program. This could be anything random, such as a computer **virus** (as in the work of Joseph Nechvatal; see the box on page 13) or the changing rhythms of the artist's heartbeat.

Perhaps the earliest example of computer-generated art was the Henry Drawing Machine. Created in 1960 by artist Desmond Paul Henry, it could generate random mathematical forms.

JOSEPH NECHVATAL

Born in Chicago, Illinois, in 1951, Joseph Nechvatal is a pioneering digital artist. In 1986, he began using computers to create paintings, and in the early 1990s, he started work on *The Computer Virus Project*. A computer virus is a piece of code that often damages or destroys data. Nechvatal introduced a computer virus into one of his digital paintings and let it transform and destroy it. During this "attack," he made new versions of the painting to show the stages of its destruction. In a second version of the project, in 2001, he displayed the attacks as a moving image on a gallery wall, so viewers could see them take place in real time.

˄ In creating his virus artworks, Joseph Nechvatal was inspired by the idea of connecting the biological (viruses) to the technological (computers).

3 PRINTMAKING

Printmaking is the process of making artworks by printing. Prints are created by transferring ink from the original artwork onto a sheet of paper or other material.

In printmaking, many copies can be made from one original. This was significant once, but less so today, when paintings can be reproduced by means of photography or digital scanning.

Woodcuts

Woodcut printmaking involves an artist drawing a design on a piece of wood and then carving away the non-image areas. The remaining surface is then inked and **impressed** on paper. This is called relief printing because the inked areas are raised above the non-inked areas. It has barely changed over the centuries, although technology has since helped to create color prints.

Engravings

Engraving is a form of intaglio printing, meaning that the raised portions of the image stay blank, while the crevices hold ink. Traditionally, a steel tool called a burin is used to cut a design into the surface of a metal plate (usually made of copper). The plate is then inked and impressed on paper using a printing press.

THE SCIENCE BEHIND: PNEUMATIC ENGRAVING TOOLS

Pneumatic tools work by air pressure, which is provided by an air compressor. This is a machine that pumps air into a steel cylinder until the air becomes pressurized. The engraving tool is connected to the cylinder with a hose. The engraving tool has a release **valve**, which opens when the user pushes a pedal or palm controller. Once the release valve is opened, pressurized air flows out of the cylinder, through the hose, and into the tool. This drives the nib through the metal.

Advances in technology have greatly helped modern engravers. Instead of pushing the burin by hand, today's engravers can use pen-shaped pneumatic engraving tools (see box). Instead of traditional steel burins, modern engraving tools have extremely hard tungsten carbide (known as "carbide") or diamond tips. Armed with such tools, the hard work of engraving in metal becomes a bit more like drawing on paper. This allows the artist to focus all of his or her attention on the design.

Laser engraving

Today, hand engraving is becoming less common in printmaking, though it is still practiced by jewelers, goldsmiths, and glass engravers. Some illustrators, however, now use laser engraving. Lasers are highly focused beams of light that can perform very accurate cutting.

The artist will create a digital scan of an illustration on a computer. The computer then directs a laser beam to cut that drawing into a surface. This will create indentations of different depths in the surface to hold the ink, ready for printing on paper.

⌄ In laser engraving, the depth of the indentation determines the lightness or darkness of the ink when it is impressed on paper.

4 SCULPTURE

Sculpture is visual art in three dimensions. People have been sculpting since prehistoric times, and artworks exist dating back to around 30,000 BCE. Like painters and printmakers, sculptors have always made use of the latest technologies, from manual tools to computers.

⌄ Artist Dawny Tootes casts sculptures using molten aluminum made from discarded cans, pots, and pans.

Traditional sculpture

For most of ancient and medieval history, sculptures were created for religious reasons, to glorify rulers and saints, and to commemorate significant events. The traditional methods of sculpture are:

- carving—using tools to shape a sculpture from a material by chipping away parts of the material
- modeling—creating a sculpture by shaping a material such as clay when it is soft and then baking it until it is hard
- casting—creating a sculpture by pouring molten metal into a mold and then allowing it to solidify
- construction—creating a sculpture by joining different materials together.

New cutting tools

The work of sculpting has become a lot easier in recent decades, thanks to technological advances and the development of power tools. Many of the cutting edges of these tools contain super-hard materials, such as carbide and diamond. These allow stone to be cut more quickly and easily.

Some power tools we use for cutting today include:

- saws—equipped with carbide or diamond teeth, saws can cut quickly and easily through stone
- drills—tools with a rotating cutting tip, used for making holes
- burrs—rotating, cylindrical tools with a rough cutting surface, used to create notches and other shapes

⌃ The abrasive saw, or cut-off saw, is a power tool that cuts hard materials such as metals. They are found mainly on building sites. They are also used by sculptors.

- angle grinders—used for cutting, grinding, and polishing
- abrasives—tools with rough surfaces used to polish a sculpture and give it a smooth, reflective surface
- plasma cutters—used for cutting metal. A gas is blown out of a nozzle at the same time an electrical current is sent through the gas. This turns some of the gas into plasma, a form of gas that is hot enough to cut through steel.

TECHNOLOGY THROUGH TIME: SCULPTING TOOLS

The traditional methods of sculpture have barely changed since ancient times. Stone carvers, for example, have always used axes to cut away unnecessary stone. Pitching tools, struck with a hammer or mallet, are used to create the rough shape, and the finer details are carved with a mallet and chisel. Further smoothing is achieved with rasps or rifflers (metal tools with rough surfaces) and sandpaper. Sculptors have continued to use these methods to this day, although many now prefer to use hand-operated power tools.

<< *Damski Czepek* by Ursula von Rydingsvard is weather-resistant because it is made out of a human-made material.

Materials through time

Many of the traditional sculpting materials we've seen have problems. Stone sculptures can last for centuries, but the material is challenging to work with: one mistake can ruin a sculpture. Bronze is hard, but not too brittle, and it picks up fine details. But it is expensive and **corrodes** over time, especially when placed outdoors. Wood is plentiful, soft, and easy to work, but it also deteriorates over time unless maintained.

New materials

Modern sculpting materials include plastics, **fiberglass**, stainless steel, and aluminum. Artists like them because they are cheap, easy to work with, long-lasting, and can have very attractive colors and textures.

You can also get synthetic (human-made) materials. Sculptors use these to create massive strong, yet light, sculptures. They can be weather resistant, easily formed into complex shapes, and can be given almost any texture. *Damski Czepek* (2006) is a large polyurethane resin sculpture by Ursula von Rydingsvard located in New York City. The artist particularly liked the translucent quality of this synthetic material.

Power tools enable sculptors to cut, shape, carve, and polish hard and **brittle** materials, including ceramic, concrete, glass, and fiberglass. They even allow artists to work with new materials, such as carbon fiber composites.

Artists who cast their sculptures are also making use of new processes, such as ceramic shell casting. This involves the following steps:

1. Make a wax **replica** of the sculpture.
2. Dip this in liquid ceramic, which hardens to create a ceramic shell.
3. Remove the wax inside the shell.
4. Fire the shell at a high heat to create a hard, strong cast.

Losing traditional skills

Advances in technology have given sculptors freedom to be creative. But if there is a downside to all this progress, it is that sculptors today are losing the centuries-old skills of hand-crafted sculpting.

With woodcarving, for example, the traditional process of working with a **gouge** or a chisel requires an understanding of the material, such as the structure of the grain. Every type of wood has its own characteristics, and the tool must be selected accordingly.

⌄ In this foundry, molten metal is being poured into a casting mold. When the metal is cool and hard, the mold is removed, revealing the cast-metal object within.

Putting it all together

There are many ways to connect different objects and materials together to create a sculpture. These include nailing, screwing, bolting, tying, and stitching. These methods have hardly changed through the centuries. However, two methods have benefited from recent advances in technology: welding and gluing.

Welding

The ability to join pieces of metal by heating them up and then hammering them together has existed since ancient times. Forge welding, as this is called, began to be replaced toward the end of the 19th century by arc welding. With this method, an electric arc is formed between a wire **electrode** and the metals. The electric arc causes the two pieces of metal to melt and join together.

By the 1930s, many artists began creating welded sculptures, including Pablo Picasso, who welded together ordinary, everyday objects, and Alexander Calder, who made welded **mobiles**. Bruce Gray is a **contemporary** sculptor who welds together pieces of scrap metal to make human figures, animals, dinosaurs, and machines. One of his most famous works is a life-size motorcycle made out of parts of a train.

⩔ Sculptor Marieke Heatwole, from Alaska, welds copper and steel to make art designed for gardens.

Hot-melt glue, sometimes called thermoplastic glue, is supplied in solid cylindrical sticks. These are inserted in the glue gun. A **heating element** melts the glue, which is pushed out of the gun's nozzle by a trigger. When it comes out of the nozzle, the glue is hot enough to burn or blister skin. As it cools, it hardens. This takes between a few seconds and a minute.

Gluing

The history of **adhesives** goes back at least 200,000 years. Glues were originally made from natural materials, such as tar, plant gum, egg, and starch. During the 19th and 20th centuries, discoveries led to the development of synthetic glues, which were more adhesive, water-resistant, and faster drying. Hot-melt glues (see above) allow sculptors to attach materials together permanently and easily in moments.

CASE STUDY / YASUAKI ONISHI

Some sculptors have found creative ways of using hot-melt glues. In Japanese artist Yasuaki Onishi's sculpture *Reverse of Volume RG*, he draped a plastic sheet over a pile of boxes, then dripped strands of hot-melt glue from the ceiling to fix the plastic in place. When the glue dried, the boxes were taken away, leaving the plastic sheet floating in mid-air, still holding the shape of the boxes. He called it *Reverse* because it seemed like the opposite of most sculptures, which are solid objects resting on the ground.

Digital sculpting

Today, many sculptors don't work directly with hand tools and materials, but design their artworks on a computer. They use digital sculpting software to create the desired shape in 3-D. This has many of the advantages of digital painting. For example, they can:

- edit the work as they go along
- erase errors
- make multiple copies of the finished sculpture
- make use of a huge palette of colors and textures.

>> This is the work of Bathsheba Grossman. The image on the right is a render that shows how one of her artworks is designed on a computer.

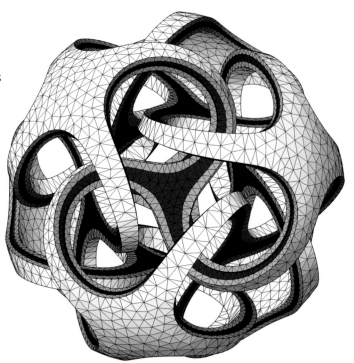

As with digital painting, sculptors can digitally sculpt work with either a mouse or a pressure-sensitive tablet and stylus. Some even use haptic devices. These are instruments that allow the artist to "feel" the sculpture while working on it, as if it were a physical object.

Sculpting with polygons

With most forms of digital sculpting, the surface of the sculpture is shown as a mesh of polygons—flat shapes with at least three straight sides. The artist can use a stylus or mouse to push and pull at these polygons, **manipulating** them into the desired position. This is the equivalent of a traditional sculptor chipping away at a block of stone.

When creating the rough shape of the sculpture, the artist works at a low resolution. In other words, the polygons are large and few in number—a thousand or less. As the work progresses and finer details are added, the artist starts to work at higher resolutions: the polygons are shrunk in size, and their number increases into the millions. The sculpture's surface starts to look much smoother and more finished.

Sculpting with voxels

Voxels are tiny, cube-shaped units, which the sculptor manipulates to achieve the desired shape. Because voxels are 3-D, the experience is more like sculpting in clay. Throughout the process, the artist is able to add and remove material.

PIONEERS

SCOTT EATON

Scott Eaton has studied drawing and sculpture, but also design and computer graphics. He is based in London, in the United Kingdom. He is a pioneer of digital sculpture, and some of his work involves creating creatures for movies and advertisements. He has recently helped develop an aged Cyclops for the movie *Wrath of the Titans*, zombies for *World War Z*, and an ogre for an advertisement. Scott works with the digital sculpting tool ZBrush, which can create very high-**resolution** models (up to a billion polygons)—this is ideal for making creatures in movies and computer games.

Making a physical copy

Some digital sculptors work in virtual reality. They create sculptures for the movie and gaming industries, so they will only ever be experienced on a screen. Others turn their work into a physical object.

- One process for this is called computer-assisted machining (CAM). Here, the computer sends instructions to a set of automated cutting tools, which then carve out the object from a block of chosen material.

- A second option is 3-D printing. This creates 3-D solid objects from a digital file. Software in the printer "slices" the digital sculpture into ultra-thin layers. A computer-directed nozzle then moves back and forth across

⌃ 3-D printing can be cheaper than CAM, but the material has to be plastic. CAM, on the other hand, can work with many different kinds of material.

a surface. It releases a liquid plastic substance that solidifies to form each of these layers, one by one. In this way, the sculpture is gradually built up, or "printed," into a solid form. In another type of 3-D printing, a laser beam moves across a container of liquid plastic. It converts the liquid to solid layers of the sculpture as it moves. Some companies offer 3-D printing with some metals and ceramics.

Sculpting with light

For years, sculptors have been looking beyond physical materials toward new mediums to manipulate. One medium that has fascinated sculptors since the 1960s is using light to create 3-D works of art. One example is Stephan Huber's *Two Horses for Münster*. To create this, Huber and his team made 3-D scans of two horses, then recreated these with layers of **neon** tubes, which emit colored light.

Japanese artist Makoto Tojiki makes sculptures using light-emitting devices called LEDs. He uses thousands of strands of LED lights to create mysterious and beautiful 3-D figures of humans, horses, and birds. Benjamin Muzzin has taken light sculpture a step further by adding movement. He placed two flat-screen monitors back to back and spun them at a very high speed. This causes a 3-D moving light form to hover in the air.

CASE STUDY / INNOVATORS IN SCULPTURE

Spanish artist Roseline de Thélin's light sculptures explore the properties of light: reflection, refraction (the splitting of light into its different parts), brightness, and transparency. She uses crystals, mirrors, Perspex (a type of solid transparent plastic), and many other materials. Aurora Robson is a Canadian artist, based in New York City, who is deeply concerned about the environment. She takes waste products such as plastic bottles and junk mail, destined for garbage dumps, and turns them into intricate sculptures, sometimes containing LED lights.

⌃ This light sculpture by Aurora Robson, called *The Quality of Mercy*, uses recycled bottles, aluminum pipe, and solar-powered fiber-optics.

5 PHOTOGRAPHY, FILM, VIDEO, AND NEW MEDIA

The invention of photography in the 19th century had a serious and long-lasting impact on the world of art. At that time, thousands of artists made their living from painting miniature portraits of people. Photography soon made this far less common. In 1830, more than 300 miniature portraits were exhibited at the Royal Academy in London. But by 1870, there were only around 30. However, could photography itself ever be accepted as art?

A fierce debate

Within two decades of its invention, some spoke of photography as a new art form. In the 1850s, Swedish artist Oscar Rejlander began experimenting with new photographic techniques that many saw as artistic. These included photomontage (placing a number of separate images into one image), double exposure (placing one image over another), and retouching (using ink or paint to change the look of a photograph).

TECHNOLOGY THROUGH TIME: EMERGENCE OF PHOTOGRAPHY

1820s: Nicéphore Niépce is the first person to successfully record images from real life on film.

1839: Louis Daguerre makes photography practical with his daguerreotype process.

1839: Invention of the **negative** allows many prints to be made.

1860s: Color photography is invented, although it will only became practical in the 1930s.

1884: Invention of photographic film means photographers no longer have to carry boxes of plates and chemicals with them, making photography more portable.

1989: The digital revolution in photography begins: the first digital camera is launched. Photos can now be digitized and saved as a computer file, making them much easier to store and manipulate.

^ This pictorialist photograph is entitled *Windowsill*. The arrangement of the objects, the lighting, the photographic technique, and the printing combine to create an artistic effect not dissimilar to that of a painting.

Despite Rejlander's efforts, many disagreed that photography was art. Some saw photography as simply a mechanical method of reproducing a scene. In reaction to this, a new movement of artist-photographers emerged in about 1885. They called themselves the pictorialists.

Pictorialism

The pictorialists manipulated photographs in order to make them seem more like handcrafted works of art. Their aim was to create works of beauty rather than merely to record facts. For example, they would:

- use a special lens to produce a softer image
- print dark parts of the photo in brown or dark blue rather than black
- use chemicals to give photos more detail or a broader range of tones
- change the texture to give an appearance of brush strokes.

Group f/64

In the early 1930s, a group of American photographers calling themselves Group f/64 formed in reaction to the pictorialists. Group f/64 believed that photography was a unique art form and not an imitation of painting or anything else. They avoided using special techniques and aimed for stark, clear images of what they observed.

Art photography today

Today, photography no longer has to fight for recognition as an art form. The top photographers are as celebrated as contemporary artists in other media, and their work is fetching high prices. A large color print of a photograph by artist Andreas Gursky called *Rhein II* sold for $4.3 million in 2011.

TECHNOLOGY THROUGH TIME: A WORLD OF PHOTOGRAPHS

Today, photographs are everywhere, and we can get almost any image we want at the touch of a button. A number of milestones have helped to bring this about:

1999: The first commercially successful camera phones are introduced.

2001: Google Image Search arrives, allowing users to search for any image online.

2003: Photoshop CS (Creative Source), a powerful image editing tool, is released.

2004: Flickr, the first specialized photo-sharing site, is launched.

2014: Photo-sharing site Instagram has 200 million users who share something each month.

Digital photography

The arrival of the digital camera in 1989 sparked an ongoing revolution in the world of art photography. Digital cameras work by storing images **electronically** rather than on light-sensitive film. And, unlike traditional cameras, they can display images immediately, on the screen in front of you.

By the early 2000s, digital cameras featured hundreds of editing tools. Photographs could be cropped, resized, flipped, sharpened, softened, and generally cleaned up. Color, tone, and brightness could all be fixed. Also, parts of an image could be changed or merged, and all with just a few clicks.

⌃ Today, editing tools such as Photoshop make it very easy for us to make improvements to photographs—for example, removing wrinkles and blemishes from a face.

The challenge to art photographers

Digital photography poses a challenge to artists, because today anyone with a smartphone can create impressively arty photos. So, what is the future for photography as an art form?

According to art photographer Liz Darlington, photographers must think about the message they are trying to convey, not just with a single shot, but with their whole body of work. According to her, "[Art lovers] want to see that photographers have a consistency of vision. That is what's lacking on these Flickr sites: lots of pretty pictures, but nothing that shows the intent of the artist."

Today's photographic artists are certainly making use of digital tools. However, this is usually as a means to enhance the ideas or emotions they are trying to convey in their work.

For example, Mike Mellia uses digital tools to create textures, light, and atmosphere that evoke the world of movies: bright, bold colors for action hero films and deep shadows for thrillers. Bryan Peterson uses the "select" tool on his digital camera to pick out certain objects in color, highlighting them in order to create a mood.

Filmmaking

In the late 1880s, French inventor Louis Le Prince developed the first camera capable of capturing motion and, with this, filmmaking was born. But filmmaking was very much a craft rather than an art at this stage, with little thought given to style.

Art films

The earliest "art" films were made in the 1920s. In *Battleship Potemkin* (1925), Russian film director Sergei Eisenstein used montage. This was the linking of several very different shots. He wanted to produce an emotional response in the audience.

In the United States, F. W. Murnau made an art film called *Sunrise: A Song of Two Humans* (1927) that used groundbreaking techniques to create an exaggerated, fairy-tale-like world. During this period, movies featured music but no other sound. This was one of the first movies to feature a soundtrack with music *and* special effects. Some effects Murnau used were:

- Dolly shots: These create smooth, gliding camera movements, created by mounting the camera on a platform (known as a dolly) and pulling it along a track.
- Forced perspective: This uses **optical illusion** to make an object appear larger or smaller than it is.

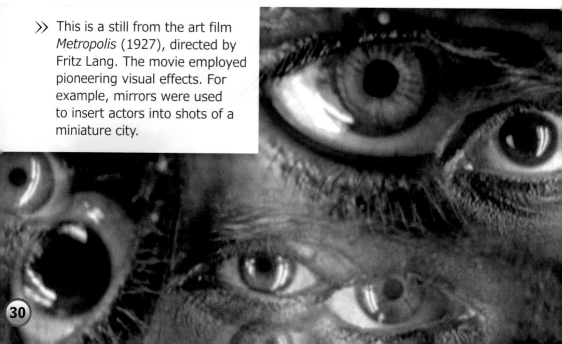

» This is a still from the art film *Metropolis* (1927), directed by Fritz Lang. The movie employed pioneering visual effects. For example, mirrors were used to insert actors into shots of a miniature city.

TECHNOLOGY THROUGH TIME: NOTABLE FILM INNOVATIONS

- The first "talkies" (films with speech) appeared in the late 1920s.
- Technicolor (a process for making color films) emerged in the early 1930s.
- The first version of 3-D films arrived in the 1950s.
- In 1976, the Steadicam was invented to create a steady tracking shot without the need for a dolly.
- In the late 1970s, computer-generated imaging (CGI) was born, opening the way for realistic animation.
- Motion capture technology, in which real actors are used to provide movements that are then recreated digitally, emerged in the early 2000s.
- In all these cases, the new techniques were pioneered by mainstream movies. Makers of art films had become much less innovative when it came to film technology. This was mainly because the technology was becoming too expensive for art films, which can have low budgets.

CASE STUDY / 2001: A SPACE ODYSSEY

One art film that did innovate was Stanley Kubrick's 1968 film *2001: A Space Odyssey*. It featured a number of novel special effects:

- Highly detailed spacecraft miniatures were carefully photographed to give the impression that they were much bigger.
- Scenes set in "outer space" were filmed using hidden wires, mirror shots, and large-scale rotating sets.
- During the climax of the movie, a new technique called "slit-scan" was used in which the image being filmed is covered except for a thin slit, which moves quickly across the image while the camera is filming. This creates unusual distorting effects.

Video: A new medium

Film was shot on reels of plastic (celluloid), but when TV arrived, it was shot as live images. It was beamed straight to people's TVs in their homes. All TV programs had to be broadcast live, except for movies.

Then, in 1956, a team at Ampex Corporation created the first practical **videotape** recorder. It captured live images from television cameras. This recorder converted the camera's electronic signals into information that could be stored on videotape.

The first video recorders were too expensive for most people. However, by the mid-1960s, the technology became cheaper and more available to artists.

⌃ American pop artist Andy Warhol was a pioneer of video art. Here he is in 1964 making an experimental movie with a more traditional medium: film.

The birth of video art

The first video artists were Nam June Paik, Juan Downey, Frank Gillette, and Andy Warhol. They all began experimenting with video in the mid-1960s.

In 1967, Sony launched the Portapak, the world's first commercially successful home videotape recorder. American artist Peter Campus used two Portapaks in his work *Double Vision* (1971). He fed video signals from the devices through an electronic **mixer**. This created distorted images, and some images often appeared on top of others.

Artists such as Stephen Beck and Nam June Paik worked with electronics experts to design tools called video synthesizers. These could control and alter video signals to produce **abstract**, often brightly colored images.

Technological advances

In the 1980s, editing technology became more widely available. Video artists, such as Gary Hill and Tony Oursler, began to add new techniques to their work, including:

- fades—slow darkening of a TV image
- wipes—when one picture seems to be wiped out by a new one
- collage—combinations of images on one screen.

The release of the first digital **camcorders** in 1995 had a major impact on video art. Digital editing software made it possible for artists to edit on home computers. Now they could make broadcast-quality videos at very low cost.

Video art today

Artists continue to produce video art, both on its own or as part of larger artworks. Some think this art form is going to change completely. This is because it is being overtaken by digital art, which offers higher quality images, more control, greater flexibility, and interactivity.

CASE STUDY / BILL VIOLA

New Yorker Bill Viola studied fine arts at Syracuse University and then worked as a video technician. His work has been described as having a "painterly quality." He often uses ultra-slow motion video to give the impression of a very slow-moving painting. In one work, *The Quintet Series*, he shows the gradually changing expressions of five actors so that every tiny change in their facial expressions can be seen.

New media art

Digital technology has changed the way we think of traditional art forms, but it is also creating new art forms that have never existed before and that are not always easy to categorize. Some people call this "new media art."

Net art

Net art is a form of new media art that is distributed via the Internet. This isn't simply art that has been digitized and placed online—it is work that relies on the Internet to exist. Net artists include:

- An Xiao, who makes conceptual artworks about social media. Her work *Morse Code Tweets* (2009) combined two technologies (**Morse code** and Twitter) to highlight the changes in the way we communicate today.
- Rafaël Rozendaal makes web sites, which he sells to collectors with the understanding that the sites must remain public, with the collector's name in the browser header. In his work *Jello Time* (2007), a gelatin mold wobbles in response to mouse movement. *Out in the Wind* (2009) causes the viewer's cursor to slowly disintegrate to a soundtrack of a howling wind.

Interactive art

Viewers of interactive art navigate, assemble, or contribute to the piece, so that each experience of the artwork is unique to that viewer. Forms of interactive art have existed since the 1920s. For example, Marcel Duchamp's *Rotary Glass Plates* (1920) required the viewer to turn on a machine and stand at a distance of about 3.5 feet (1 meter) to see an optical illusion.

PIONEERS

MAURICE BENAYOUN

In Maurice Benayoun's *The Tunnel Under the Atlantic* (1995), a 6.6-feet (2-meter) diameter tube rose out of the floor of two museums: one in Montreal, Canada; the other in Paris, France. Visitors in each museum were invited to use a joystick device to "dig" through the tube to create a virtual tunnel connecting the two cities. Instead of digging earth, they found layers of images from the history of French and Canadian culture. While digging, they could talk to diggers at the other end of the "tunnel."

INTERACTIVE ART IN THE DIGITAL AGE

Interactive art has been given a new focus today, thanks to digital technology. Some digital artworks have used **sensors** that determine things such as the viewer's motion and distance.

In Chris Milk's *The Treachery of Sanctuary* (2012), you, the viewer, stand in front of a series of white screens. In the first screen, your silhouetted body slowly dissolves into birds, which fly away. In the second, birds swoop down and snatch pieces of you away. In the third, your arms turn into giant wings, and if you flap them, you fly away. Similarly, *Nothing to Tweet Home About* (2009) is a series of status updates sent in the form of postcards.

Penelope Umbrico also uses her art to comment on social media. Her ongoing work *Suns from Flickr* (begun in 2006) uses hundreds of photos of sunsets found on Flickr, cropped and put together in a single image.

⌃ Viewers spread their wings before *The Treachery of Sanctuary* by Chris Milk at the Barbican's "Digital Revolution" exhibition in London.

ART IN THE AGE OF THE INTERNET

6

Modern technology has not only changed the way artists work, it has also broken down barriers between artists and the general public. Thanks to the Internet and social media, art lovers can now connect with their favorite artists, and artists with their audience.

Getting past the gatekeepers

Traditionally, the most powerful people in the art world were gallery owners, patrons (financial supporters), collectors, and professional art critics. These are the "gatekeepers," who decided which artists were good and which weren't. Until recently, if these individuals weren't interested in an artist, the artist's work had no chance of being exhibited or bought.

But in the age of the Internet, artists can present their work directly to the public on their web sites and social media. As a result, the traditional gatekeepers of the art world have lost a lot of their power.

⌄ Photographers show their work at a fine art photography show in Santa Monica, California. These events remain popular, but artists can reach far more people using the Internet and social media.

Crowdfunding

But how do artists earn a living without the support of wealthy patrons? The Internet can help here, too. Crowdfunding is a way of raising money for a project by asking for financial contributions from a large number of people. Some donate money because they wish to see the artist's work. Others may be tempted by a reward, such as an autographed print.

Internet crowdfunding began in 2003 with ArtistShare, a web site that invites fans of musical artists to fund their projects. Soon, similar web sites were launched, the biggest being Kickstarter. Between 2009, when it began, and 2014, Kickstarter raised over $58 million in pledges for more than 20,000 projects related to the visual arts.

Breaking down the barriers

Thanks to technology, more people are creating their own art and sharing it with the world. But because it is easier to create art, there is more "bad art" out there. However, the new tools also mean that the really talented artists are able to experiment in completely new directions.

Many of today's artists are very at ease with the world of social media. They may blog and tweet about their day-to-day experiences, in addition to announcing forthcoming events and exhibitions.

Selling art online

The Internet provides a huge opportunity for artists to sell their work. In 2013, online sales came to just 1.6 percent of total global art sales. However, this is set to rise thanks to a recent, huge expansion in Internet-based art sellers, including Artspace, ArtGallery, Paddle8, and Amazon Art.

CASE STUDY / DIGITAL ART FOR SALE

In addition to offering a storefront for traditional art, the Internet is also the place to sell digital art. A web site called s[edition] sells limited edition digital artworks. "Limited edition" means that only a certain number of copies of that artwork will ever be sold, which makes it much more likely that the artwork will gain in value.

For example, s[edition] sold 2,000 digital photos of Damien Hirst's diamond-studded baby skull, *For Heaven's Sake*, for $800. They also sold 2,000 of Tracey Emin's *Love Is What You Want* (a work written in neon) for just $80 (the original is worth around $50,000).

Once bought, the work is delivered to the buyer, along with a certificate of authenticity signed by the artist. This allows the buyer to sell the piece, if desired, should the price of the work rise. The buyer can download the artwork to a smartphone, tablet, or computer.

SAATCHI ONLINE

Charles Saatchi is a famous British art collector. He owns a gallery in London (see picture, right), which showcases both established and up-and-coming modern artists. He also owns an innovative art web site, Saatchi Online. The site offers new artists:

- the chance to display and sell their work, whether or not they are represented by another gallery

- global, year-round exposure, instead of only during periods when, and in places where, they have an exhibition

- a larger percentage of the sales proceeds than usual (most art dealers take around 50 percent of sales proceeds, while Saatchi Online takes 30 percent).

Saatchi Online offers art consumers:

- access to artworks from up-and-coming artists from around the globe

- artworks that have been carefully selected for quality before being displayed online

- an "art advisory service" to help art collectors decide what to buy.

Yet there remains some resistance to buying art on the Internet. According to a 2013 report, 79 percent of people who did *not* buy art online said it was because they couldn't inspect the artwork before they were able to purchase the art. It is therefore likely that artists will continue to display their work in galleries and at exhibitions in the "offline world," too.

7 ART, TECHNOLOGY, AND CRIME

Although digital technology offers many benefits to artists, it also poses a threat. For example, it has made it much easier for people to use, alter, and distribute an artist's work without permission.

Misuse of artwork

Digital artwork (or traditional artwork that has been scanned and digitized), once placed on the Internet, can be downloaded by anyone and used in any way they choose. People can crop, edit, change, or add to artwork. They can print out hundreds of copies and use it to sell a product or promote a political cause—and they often don't ask for the artist's permission.

Copyright

Copyright laws help to protect artists from having other people use their artwork without permission. The laws state that artists alone have the right to use their artwork as they want. If a person uses an artist's work without permission, that person is "in breach of copyright" and can be taken to court by the artist.

⩔ Artists can help protect themselves against copyright infringement by watermarking digital images of their work.

In practice, however, copyright laws are hard to enforce: the Internet is huge, and it is almost impossible for artists to keep track of their work. Instead, artists can take the following steps to protect their art:

- Upload only low-resolution files of their artwork to web sites (low-res files look fuzzy when printed)
- Watermark images of their artwork (this means they can place a faint logo over the image to make people not want to use it)
- Disable right-clicking on their web site, so people can't copy images onto their desktops
- Officially register copyright in the work (artists automatically have copyright for any work they create, but registering copyright gives an added layer of protection)
- Edit the metadata (the information that all digital files contain, stating things like file size and date created) on images of artwork to identify the artist and state that he/she is the copyright owner
- Keep their contact information up to date and visible on their web site, so no one can later claim "we couldn't find the owner to ask permission."

PIONEERS

CREATIVE COMMONS

An organization called Creative Commons (CC), set up in 2001, offers a more flexible form of copyright for the Internet Age. CC has created a range of **licenses**, which artists can offer those who wish to use their work. The most flexible of these allow people to edit or add to the artwork and use it for themselves or to sell something, as long as the artist is **credited**. The most restrictive license allows people to download and share this work, crediting the artist. There are restrictions. They agree not to change the work in any way, and not use it to sell anything.

Selling fakes online

The Internet has increased the sale of fake works of art. Today, there are web sites selling "genuine" works by masters such as Rembrandt, Matisse, and Picasso for as little as $500. These works are clearly fakes, yet people are buying them. Fakes can take three main forms:

1. Unauthorized copies that breach the artist's copyright
2. Authorized copies containing the artist's forged signature, turning a cheap print into an expensive "signed" limited edition
3. Forged, or faked, works of art.

》 The brooch on the right is around 2,500 years old. It was stolen in 2006 and replaced with the fake (left).

CASE STUDY / FAKE JACKSON POLLOCKS

In 2005, a team of scientists used Raman spectroscopy to examine 19 paintings, supposedly by the American artist Jackson Pollock (1912–1956)—paintings that had already been **authenticated** by a Pollock expert. The scientists discovered that the works included five paint pigments that didn't exist when Pollock was alive, proving that they were fakes.

⌃ Thanks to X-rays, this "ancient Egyptian" cat sculpture, on display at New York City's Metropolitan Museum of Art, was exposed as a fake.

Technology to the rescue

Forgers often go to great lengths to create fake paintings, such as dipping paintings in chemicals to make them appear older. Some people even drill fake holes in the frame. Today, investigators can use a range of techniques to examine a painting to test whether it is genuine. Tests include:

- Microscope testing: By magnifying the surface of a painting by up to 50 times, experts can check whether the craquelure (the network of fine cracks that appear after the passage of time) is genuine. For example, analysis of the painting *The Virgin and the Child with an Angel* by Francesco Francia (1450–1517) revealed that some of the craquelure was created by pencil, suggesting that it is a fake.
- UV light testing: When an old painting is bathed in **ultraviolet (UV) light**, the varnish will glow brightly. If the areas have been recently retouched, they will glow weakly or not at all.
- X-ray: By X-raying a painting, investigators can see if there is a painting beneath it. If there is, and it appears more modern than the top painting, it suggests that the top painting is a fake.
- Raman spectroscopy: With this method, a laser beam is aimed at the surface of a painting. When the beam strikes **molecules** on the surface, some of its light is scattered in unique patterns. This depends upon which chemicals it strikes. Scientists can figure out from these patterns the makeup of the paint that was used. This tells them the time period the paint came from.

8 THE FUTURE OF ART

Technology is likely to continue changing the way we create art, just as it has throughout history. As new equipment and techniques are developed, artists will be inspired to find ever more inventive ways of stimulating people's senses. So, what trends of today can give us a clue about the future of art?

⤒ This work by Angela Easterling, called *Fairy with Feather*, is a photogram—a photographic image made without a camera. Photograms are made by placing objects directly onto a light-sensitive material and then exposing it to light.

New art forms

Art is changing. Modern artists no longer feel restricted to traditional media, such as painting, sculpture, and photography. For example:

- Ollie Palmer collaborated with scientists to create an "ant ballet." Together, they developed an artificial **pheromone**, which Palmer used to direct the movements of the ants to create a kind of dance.
- Luke Jerram used highly magnified photographs of viruses as his models, then sculpted them out of glass.
- Hugh Turvey created art from colored X-ray photographs.

THE SCIENCE BEHIND: 3-D DISPLAYS

The 3-D display device is made up of a transparent screen with tiny light sources, LEDs, around the edges. Light rays from the LEDs are sent toward the center of the screen. These rays strike pixels (minute areas of illumination) that steer the light out of the screen in different directions. Through careful control of the light, the device sends slightly different images to each eye. These images are combined in the brain to create a 3-D object.

In 2013, scientists managed to create a glasses-free, 3-D image that can be viewed from different angles. It looks just like a statue made of light. The technology may one day work on a cell phone.

Will video games become an art form?

As we've seen, photography struggled for recognition as an art form in the mid- to late 19th century. Video games have faced a long battle to be treated as something more than just entertainment since their emergence in the 1970s.

To this day, there are many who would say that a video game isn't art. Film critic Roger Ebert said: "One obvious difference between art and games is that you can win a game. It has rules, points, objectives, and an outcome."

Yet it would appear that attitudes are changing. In 2011, the U.S. Supreme Court ruled that video games should be considered art. In 2013, New York City's Museum of Modern Art hosted an exhibition of video game classics, such as SimCity2000, Tetris, and Pac-Man.

Today, there is a whole genre known as "art games," created to provoke an emotional reaction in users. *That Dragon, Cancer* (2014), created by game designer Ryan Green, is about a family coping with the discovery that their son is going to die. It is based on Green's own experiences.

New ways to enjoy art

Technology not only influences what art is made, but also how it is displayed and appreciated. For example, what about turning the walls of our homes into giant canvases for art? They could display digitally rendered landscapes or a virtual 3-D relief carving.

And it's likely that we'll be able to shape the art in our homes, too. At the touch of a cell phone or a spoken command, we'll be able to alter the scenes on our walls, or even the holographic light sculpture on our coffee table, to suit our moods.

This future may not be so far away. A company called Framed is already offering high-definition, framed screens that can display countless images, videos, animations, and graphics. With the aid of an app, users can transfer artworks from all over the Internet straight to their walls.

Our ability to shape the art we see around us doesn't need to end when we step out of our front door. With wearable technology, such as Google Glass, we'll even be able to edit the art we encounter in galleries or on the street.

CASE STUDY / 3-D PRINTING

It's too early to say how this new, flexible technology (see page 24) might be used by artists. People already print their artworks. A 2014 installation by Karsten Schmidt included a huge, funnel-shaped 3-D printed structure. The structure surrounded a 3-D printer, allowing visitors to design and print their own art.

As 3-D printers get cheaper, artists could create works as a digital file for buyers to print out for themselves at home. Some are already doing that. Artist and designer Don Foley has created a 3-D printing project for a picture frame, complete with pipes, cogs, and fantasy technology.

3-D printing may one day turn all of us into designers and artists. Imagine being able to design your own personalized computer mouse, phone case, or jewelry!

TECHNOLOGY THROUGH TIME: 3-D PRINTING

1984: Chuck Hull of 3-D Systems Corp invents a 3-D printing process called stereolithography.

Late 1980s: Industry begins to use 3-D printing to create prototypes, or the first physical versions, of new designs.

1990: Stratasys, Ltd., begin commercially manufacturing 3-D printers under the name Fused Deposition Modeling (FDM).

Early 1990s: The Massachusetts Institute of Technology (MIT) develops a system that it calls 3-D printing (3-DP). The name sticks.

2013: The first 3-D printers for home use go on sale. Mac Bogue creates the 3-Doodler—the world's first 3-D drawing pen.

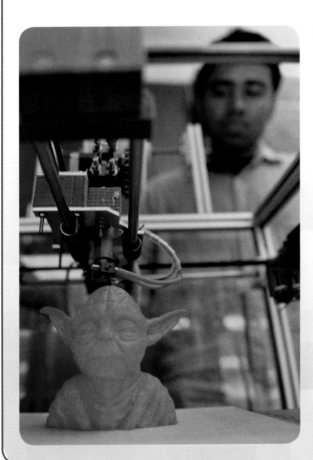

≪ The *Star Wars* character Yoda is printed on a portable 3-D printer. In the future, these devices could be in every home, allowing us to design and print our own personalized art.

The artificial artist

In the future, not all artists may be human. Impressive art is already being created by machines. For example, a computer program called AARON, created by artist and software developer Harold Cohen, can paint pictures of people, plants, trees, and simple objects with no human input.

Computers as artists in their own right

AARON shows that computer programs can learn and decide things. They can make paintings and other objects that have never existed in any human's imagination.

Unlike human artists, computers do not yet set out to make art—they're programmed to do so. Some people say that this proves they are not artists—the "real" artists are the programmers. By this argument, computers are simply sophisticated tools. But time will tell whether these "tools" will become artists in their own right.

⌃ We still view artists as people who use tools, from paint palettes to computers, to create art. But what if computers become the artists?

Technology is invaluable

Some people think there may be a danger of overreliance on technology. It can lead to artwork that might look too perfect, lacking the imperfections that mark it out as the work of a human being. Technology is an invaluable tool for making art, but they think the artist should always be ultimately in charge.

But we have seen that today, art and technology are combining as never before. Artists are teaming up with scientists and engineers to create new wonders to move, delight, and disturb. The digital revolution has breathed fresh life into traditional media, and it is also inspiring artists to create brand new art forms.

CASE STUDY / THE PAINTING FOOL

The computer program the Painting Fool, created by Dr. Simon Colton in 2001, paints portraits of people from photographs. It can vary the colors and style of its paintings, depending on how it interprets the sitter's mood. For example, if it views that its subject is happy, it will paint in a carefree style with bright colors. A sad expression on its subject's face will prompt it to paint in muted colors. The Painting Fool does this because it is linked up to software that locates faces within an image and recognizes some facial expressions, such as smiling and frowning.

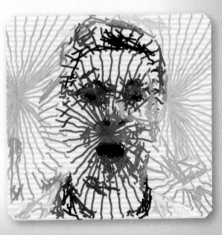

TIMELINE

1822: Nicéphore Niépce creates the first fixed photographic image

1839: Louis Daguerre announces his daguerreotype process for creating detailed permanent photographs on silver-plated sheets of copper

1840: John Herschel makes the first glass negative, allowing many prints to be made of one photograph

1861: James Clerk Maxwell creates the first durable color photograph

1878: Eadweard Muybridge makes the first motion picture sequence—of a man on a galloping horse

1884: Photographic film is invented

1885: Pictorialism, a movement dedicated to the promotion of photography as an art form, emerges

1888: Louis Le Prince develops the first movie camera and films the world's first motion picture, *Roundhay Garden Scene*

1925: Sergei Eisenstein makes *Battleship Potemkin*, an early art film

1956: A team at Ampex Corporation invents the first practical videotape recorder

1960: Desmond Paul Henry creates the Henry Drawing Machine, which produced the first computer-generated art

1963: Ivan Sutherland creates Sketchpad, the world's first computer illustration program

1965: Nam June Paik creates the first example of video art

1967: Sony releases the Portapak, the first commercially successful home videotape recorder

1968: RAND introduces the first commercially successful graphics tablet

1973: Artist and software developer Harold Cohen creates AARON, the artificial artist. AARON has been in continual development ever since.

1984: Apple launches MacPaint, an early digital painting program

1987: Adobe launches Illustrator, allowing artists and designers to create and edit shapes and images and to manipulate text

1989: Fujifilm releases the Fuji DS-X, the world's first digital camera

1990: Adobe launches Photoshop, allowing artists and designers to edit and manipulate photographs and illustrations

1995: Sony and others introduce DV, a format for storing digital video, signaling the birth of the digital camcorder

1995: Artist Vuk Cosic comes up with the term "net.art" to describe a growing movement of artists who rely on the Internet both as a platform and as subject matter for their work

2001: Creative Commons is launched, with the aim of making it easier for artists to share their work without fear of being exploited

2001: Dr. Simon Colton develops his art-creating computer program, the Painting Fool

2002: Pixologic Inc. releases the first version of the digital sculpting software, ZBrush

2010: Saatchi Online, a virtual gallery and storefront for emerging artists, launches

2011: *Rhein II*, a photograph by artist Andreas Gursky, becomes the most highly priced photograph in the world when it is sold at **auction** for $4.3 million

2011: [s]edition starts selling limited edition works of art in a digital format

2013: Amazon starts selling original works of art

2013: New York's Museum of Modern Art hosts an exhibition of video games

2013: Maplin releases the first 3-D printers for home use

2014: "Digital Revolutions," an exhibition at London's Barbican Centre, showcases the latest in interactive digital art

2014: Kickstarter, the crowdfunding site, hosts its first ever art show

GLOSSARY

abstract relating to ideas, as opposed to physical reality

adhesive substance used for sticking things together. Glue is an adhesive.

airbrush artist's device for spraying paint using compressed air

auction public sale in which goods are sold to the highest bidder

authentic real or genuine, not fake

authenticated showed that something is true and genuine—for example, that a painting is the work of a particular artist

binder substance used to stick, or bind, things together

brittle hard but likely to break or shatter easily

camcorder portable combined video camera and video recorder

chisel long-bladed hand tool with a beveled (sloped) cutting edge

collaborated worked on a team with others on an activity

commission order the production of something, such as a work of art

conceptual art in which the idea presented by the artist is as important as, if not more important than, the finished product

contemporary living or occurring at the same time

corrode destroy or damage something slowly, usually by a chemical reaction

credited clearly acknowledged as the creator of a work

digitize convert into a digital form that can be processed by a computer

electrode conductor that passes an electrical current from a power source to a material

electronic describing a device that works by means of small parts that control and direct an electric current

exclusive restricted or limited to one person

fiberglass tough plastic material made of glass fibers that are put in resin

format form, design, or arrangement of something

gouge chisel with a concave (curved-in) blade

graphics design or illustration

heating element strip of metal or a wire that converts electricity into heat

impressed made a mark or design on an object using, for example, a stamp or printing press

laser device that generates an intense beam of light

license legal permission, usually in writing, from the owner of something you wish to use

manipulate handle or control a tool or creative medium, such as clay, in a skilled way

manual done with the hands

mixer device for merging input signals to create a combined output

mobile decorative structure that is suspended (hung) so that it can turn freely in the air

molecule group of atoms that are bonded together

Morse code code in which letters are represented by combinations of long and short signals of light or sound. It was used as a means of transmitting messages by telegraph before the invention of the telephone.

negative photographic image made on film or glass that shows the light and shade or color values reversed from the original, and from which positive prints can be made

neon fluorescent lighting (neon is a gaseous element that is often used in such lighting)

optical illusion something that deceives the eye

palette range of colors available to a user

pheromone chemical released by an animal, affecting the behavior of others of its species

physical having material existence, such as a painting on canvas or a stone sculpture

pigment substance that gives color to paint, dye, or ink

pixel tiny area of illumination on a display screen

replica exact copy of something, usually to a smaller scale

resolution degree of detail visible in a photograph or video image

sensor device that detects or measures movements or changes in nearby objects

stylus pen-like device used to input text or drawings into a computer by making impressions on a touch-sensitive tablet or screen

ultraviolet (UV) light light with a wavelength shorter than visible light but longer than that of X-rays

valve device for controlling the passage of fluid through a pipe

videotape tape for recording and reproducing visual images and sound

virtual reality computer-generated simulation of a 3-D image or environment

virus in computers, a destructive program; in medicine, a microscopic germ that can cause disease in humans and animals

Find Out More

Books

Dickins, Rosie. *The Usborne Introduction to Modern Art*. New York: Scholastic, 2006.

Gaines, Thom. *Digital Photo Madness!* New York: Lark, 2010.

Heine, Florian. *13 Art Inventions Children Should Know*. New York: Prestel, 2011.

Make Art, Make Mistakes: A Creativity Sketchbook (MoMA Modern Kids). San Francisco: Chronicle, 2010.

Miles, Liz. *Movie Special Effects* (Culture in Action). Chicago: Raintree, 2010.

Web sites

Use FactHound to find Internet sites related to this book. All of the sites on FactHound have been researched by our staff.

Here's all you do:
Visit *www.facthound.com*
Type in this code: 9781484626399

Movies

Battleship Potemkin (Sergei Eisenstein, 1925)
This is a dramatized account of a great Russian naval mutiny and a resulting street demonstration. It is one of the earliest art films.

Citizen Kane (Orson Welles, 1941)
This is an amazing movie about a newspaper tycoon, which uses many pioneering cinematic techniques.

Further research

1. Visit a gallery, museum, or any place where art is exhibited. Try to figure out the techniques that were used to create the art on display. If possible, speak to the person who has organized the exhibition (the curator), or see what you can find out from the artists' web sites.

2. Why not try creating some digital artwork of your own? Use a phone or tablet to take a photo or video and then use filters and other effects to create something unique. Remember to think like an artist: before you start, ask yourself what your intention is. What reaction are you trying to create in the viewer? When you have finished, ask yourself how close you got to your original vision. Sometimes great art happens by accident and has nothing to do with what you first intended. Even so, it helps to start with a plan.

3. Choose an artist who works with modern technology. He or she could be someone mentioned in this book, or someone else you've heard of. See what you can find out about the artist on the Internet, then write a brief biography. Include information on the following: What were the artist's early influences? Does the artist have a background in science and technology? How does the artist work with technology? What do you particularly admire about the artist's work?

INDEX